Sacagawea

Published in the United States of America by Cherry Lake Publishing
Ann Arbor, Michigan
www.cherrylakepublishing.com

Content Adviser: Ryan Emery Hughes, Doctoral Student, School of Education, University of Michigan
Reading Adviser: Marla Conn, ReadAbility, Inc.
Book Design: Jennifer Wahi
Illustrator: Jeff Bane

Photo Credits: © Denton Rumsey/Shutterstock Images, 5; © The Voyageur's Paddle, illus. by David Geister
(Sleeping Bear Press), 7; © Library of Congress, 9, 22; © P is for Potato: An Idaho Alphabet, illus. by Jocelyn Slack
(Sleeping Bear Press), 11; © Yongyut Kumsri/Shutterstock Images, 13; © Joseph Sohm/Shutterstock Images, 15;
© E is for Evergreen: A Washington State Alphabet, illus. by Linda Holt Ayriss (Sleeping Bear Press), 17, 23; ©
nicoolay/istockphoto.com, 19; © Neftali/Shutterstock Images, 21; Cover, 4, 10, 14, Jeff Bane; Various frames
throughout, Shutterstock Images

Library of Congress Cataloging-in-Publication Data

Haldy, Emma E.
  Sacagawea / by Emma E. Haldy ; illustrated by Jeff Bane.
    pages cm -- (My itty-bitty bio)
  Includes bibliographical references and index.
  ISBN 978-1-63470-482-3 (hardcover) -- ISBN 978-1-63470-542-4 (pdf) -- ISBN 978-1-63470-602-5 (pbk.) -- ISBN
978-1-63470-662-9 (ebook)
 1. Sacagawea--Juvenile literature. 2. Shoshoni women--Biography--Juvenile literature. 3. Shoshoni Indians--
Biography--Juvenile literature. 4. Lewis and Clark Expedition (1804-1806)--Juvenile literature. I. Bane, Jeff, 1957-
illustrator. II. Title.

 F592.7.S123H35 2016
 978.0049745740092--dc23
 [B]

                                    2015026237

Printed in the United States of America
Corporate Graphics

2

About the author: Emma E. Haldy is a former librarian and a proud Michigander. She lives with her husband, Joe, and an ever-growing collection of books.

About the illustrator: Jeff Bane and his two business partners own a studio along the American River in Folsom California, home of the 1849 gold Rush. When Jeff's not sketching or illustrating for clients, he's either swimming or kayaking in the river to relax.

I was born near a river. I was named "Bird Woman."

My family was **Native American.**

4

I was taken from my family.

I lived with another **tribe**.

I married a fur trader.

Two men named Lewis and Clark came to my village. They were **explorers**.

They hired my husband to help them.

What part of the world would you
like to explore? Why?

They wanted my help, too. I agreed to join them.

I brought my baby son with me.

I knew how to speak to my people. I could talk for Lewis and Clark.

Along the way, we met my brother. He helped us get horses and a guide.

I also helped by making clothes and shoes.

I gathered food.
I knew which
plants we could eat.

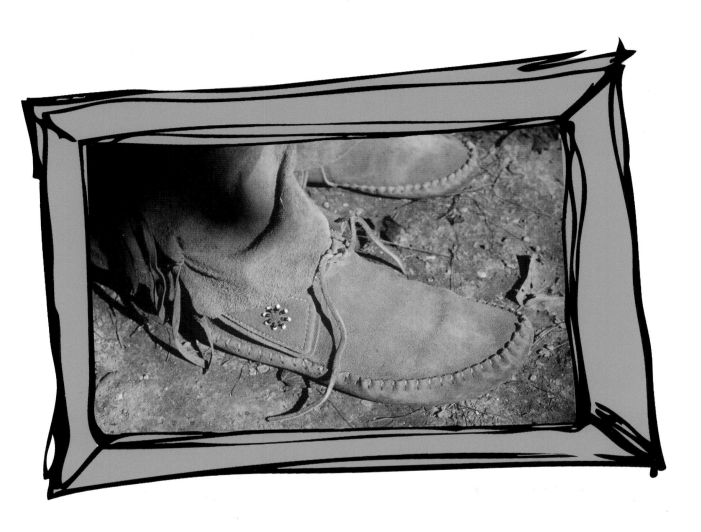

We went down rivers. We went across mountains.

After months, we reached the ocean. I saw a beached whale.

What would you want to see
at the ocean? Why?

When the trip was over, I went home.

Lewis and Clark became famous for their work.

19

I died a few years later. Clark adopted my son.

I was an amazing woman. I helped Lewis and Clark explore the West.

What would you like to ask me?

1804

1780

Born
1788

Died
1812

1805

1880

glossary

explorers (ik-SPLOR-urhz) people who discover places

Native American (NAY-tiv uh-MER-i-kuhn) one of the people who originally lived in America, or a relative of these people

tribe (TRIBE) a large group of related people who live in the same area

index

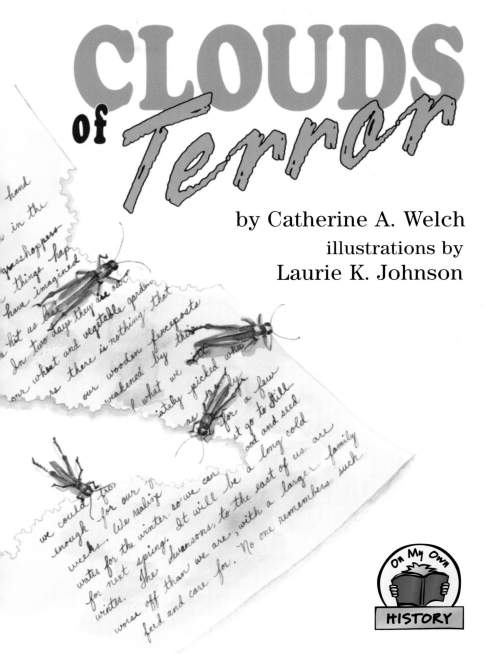

CLOUDS of Terror

by Catherine A. Welch

illustrations by
Laurie K. Johnson

Millbrook Press/Minneapolis

To my parents and brothers —C. A. W.
For Larry — who always believed in me —L. K. J.

The author wishes to thank the following people and organizations for their help in gathering material for this book: staff of the Monroe (Connecticut) Public Library; Minnesota Historical Society; U. S. Department of Agriculture; Wheat Quality Council; German from Russia Historical Society.

Text copyright © 1994 by Catherine A. Welch
Illustrations copyright © 1994 by Lerner Publishing Group, Inc.

This book is available in two editions:
Library binding by Millbrook Press,
    a division of Lerner Publishing Group, Inc.
Soft cover by First Avenue Editions,
    an imprint of Lerner Publishing Group, Inc.
241 First Avenue North, Minneapolis, MN 55401 U.S.A.

Website address: www.lernerbooks.com

Welch, Catherine A.
    Clouds of terror / Catherine A. Welch: illustrations by
Laurie K. Johnson.
        p. cm. — (Carolrhoda on my own books)
        Summary: Living on a farm in southwestern Minnesota in the 1870's,
a brother and sister try to help their family cope with plagues of locusts.
    ISBN-13: 978-0-87614-771-9 (lib. bdg. : alk. paper)
    ISBN-10: 0-87614-771-6 (lib. bdg. : alk. paper)
    ISBN-13: 978-0-87614-639-2 (pbk. : alk. paper)
    ISBN-10: 0-87614-639-6 (pbk. : alk. paper)
    [1. Frontiers and pioneer life—Minnesota—Fiction. 2. Minnesota—
Fiction. 3. Grasshoppers—Fiction.] I. Johnson, Laurie K., ill. II.
Title. III. Series: Carolrhoda on my own book.
PZ7.W4486C1   1994
[E]—dc20   93-18416

Manufactured in the United States of America
9 – JR – 10/1/11